Wilde Words

edited by Erica Gerald Mason

Wilde Words

©Erica Gerald Mason
Cover Photo by tolgatezcan/Dollar Photo Club

Wilde Words

To: Hannah
From: Mrs. Arjona

The Importance of Being Earnest
March 2016

"Hey... did I ever tell you the peanut joke?"
:)

Wilde Words

Introduction

Are you seeking a new method of journaling? Are you ready to live your best life now? Looking for an unusual way to meditate? Then this journal is for you.

Wilde Words is a written meditation series based on works and words from the famed author, Oscar Wilde. The journal is a guidebook of thoughtful quotes as writing prompts, carefully chosen to inspire creative writing, journaling and written meditation.

The act of journaling can spark transformation, self-love and

---

Wilde Words

acceptance. This guide is a snappy, fun and unexpected practice to unveil the answer to the age old question: "how do I become a better person?" Writing prompts designed for self reflection broaden your insight into the realization of who you really are. This awareness holds up a mirror to your soul, and tells you how beautiful you are, just the way you are, in this moment. Your only task is to open your heart, quiet your mind, and release your preconceived notions of meditations.

Wilde Words

Once you make this shift in your consciousness then, your intentions change. When we change our intentions, we change our world. You'll begin to notice these shifts, almost as if they were tectonic plates rearranging themselves right before your eyes....and then, something beautiful happens: your path with begin to reveal itself to you.

Wilde Words

"If you cannot think well, others will do your thinking for you."

Wilde Words

"The great events of the world take place in the brain..."

Wilde Words

"Be yourself; everyone else is already taken."

Wilde Words

"She behaves as if she was beautiful. Most American women do. It is the secret of their charm."

Wilde Words

"Moderation is a fatal thing. Nothing succeeds like excess."

Wilde Words

"To love oneself is the beginning of a lifelong romance."

Wilde Words

"When the Gods wish to punish us, they answer our prayers."

Wilde Words

"Some things are more precious because they don't last long."

Wilde Words

"Every woman is a rebel."

Wilde Words

"Conformity is the last refuge of the unimaginative"

Wilde Words

"Keep love in your heart. A life without it is like a sunless garden when the flowers are dead."

Wilde Words

"Always forgive your enemies; nothing annoys them so much."

Wilde Words

"Wisdom comes with winters"

Wilde Words

"They get up early, because they have so much to do, and go to bed early, because they have so little to think about."

Wilde Words

"Fashion is a form of ugliness so intolerable that we have to alter it every six months."

Wilde Words

"Always! That is a dreadful word. It makes me shudder when I hear it."

Wilde Words

"With freedom, books, flowers, & the moon, who couldn't be happy?"

Wilde Words

"Only the shallow know themselves"

Wilde Words

"I choose my friends for their good looks, my acquaintances for their good characters, and my enemies for their good intellects."

Wilde Words

"It is perfectly monstrous,' he said, at last, 'the way people go about nowadays saying things against one behind one's back that are absolutely and entirely true."

Wilde Words

"Man can believe the impossible, but can never believe the improbable"

Wilde Words

"I am so clever that sometimes I don't understand a single word of what I am saying."

Wilde Words

"To live is the rarest thing in the world. Most people exist, that is all."

Wilde Words

"Society often forgives the criminal; it never forgives the dreamer."

Wilde Words

"A flower blossoms for its own joy."

Wilde Words

"To become a spectator of one's own life is to escape the suffering of life."

Wilde Words

"I don't regret for a single moment having lived for pleasure.

Wilde Words

"Every single human being should be the fulfilment of a prophecy."

Wilde Words

"I adore simple pleasures. They are the last refuge of the complex."

Wilde Words

"Hear no evil, speak no evil, and you won't be invited to cocktail parties."

Wilde Words

"The world's a stage and the play is badly cast."

Wilde Words

"One should always play fairly when one has the winning cards."

Wilde Words

"A man who takes himself too seriously will find that no one else takes him seriously."

Wilde Words

"A passion for pleasure is the secret of remaining young."

Wilde Words

"To define is to limit."

Wilde Words

"I can resist anything except temptation."

Wilde Words

"But she is happiest alone. She is happiest alone."

Wilde Words

"I don't say we all ought to misbehave. But we ought to look as if we could"

Wilde Words

"There is only one thing in the world worse than being talked about, and that is not being talked about."

Wilde Words

"Selfishness is not living as one wishes to live, it is asking others to live as one wishes to live."

Wilde Words

"Only dull people are brilliant at breakfast."

Wilde Words

"We are all in the gutter, but some of us are looking at the stars."

Wilde Words

"I like persons better than principles, and I like persons with no principles better than anything else in the world."

"If one cannot enjoy reading a book over and over again, there is no use in reading it at all."

Wilde Words

"It is what you read when you don't have to that determines what you will be when you can't help it."

Wilde Words

"I beg your pardon I didn't recognise you - I've changed a lot."

Wilde Words

"Illusion is the first of all pleasures"

Wilde Words

"You are what you read."

Wilde Words

"Life is not complex. We are complex. Life is simple, and the simple thing is the right thing."

Wilde Words

"Friendship is far more tragic than love. It lasts longer."

Wilde Words

"The public is wonderfully tolerant. It forgives everything except genius."

Wilde Words

"He wanted to be where no one would know who he was. He wanted to escape from himself."

Wilde Words

"I was working on the proof of one of my poems all the morning, and took out a comma. In the afternoon I put it back again."

Wilde Words

"No good deed goes unpunished."

Wilde Words

"She is all the great heroines of the world in one."

Wilde Words

"She is more than an individual."

Wilde Words

"Wickedness is a myth invented by good people to account for the curious attractiveness of others."

Wilde Words

"To deny one's own experiences is to put a lie into the lips of one's own life. It is no less than a denial of the soul."

Wilde Words

"A writer is someone who has taught his mind to misbehave."

Wilde Words

"What does it profit a man if he gain the whole world and lose his own soul?"

Wilde Words

"We are each our own devil, and we make this world our hell."

Wilde Words

"The world was my oyster but I used the wrong fork."

Wilde Words

"A pessimist is somebody who complains about the noise when opportunity knocks."

Wilde Words

"The mystery of love is greater than the mystery of death."

Wilde Words

"We live in an age when unnecessary things are our only necessities."

Wilde Words

"A true artist takes no notice whatever of the public. The public are to him non-existent"

Wilde Words

"The Book of Life begins with a man and a woman in a garden. It ends with Revelations."

Wilde Words

"Some cause happiness wherever they go; others whenever they go."

Wilde Words

"Surely love is a wonderful thing. It is more precious than emeralds, and dearer than fine opals. Pearls and pomegranates cannot buy it..."

Wilde Words

"Whenever people agree with me I always feel I must be wrong."

Wilde Words

"Life is far too important a thing ever to talk seriously about."

Wilde Words

"Every impulse we strangle will only poison us."

Wilde Words

"I represent to you all the sins you have never had the courage to commit."

Wilde Words

"The basis of optimism is sheer terror."

Wilde Words

"She had a passion for secrecy, but she herself was merely a Sphinx without a secret."

"Where there is sorrow, there is holy ground."

Wilde Words

"The final mystery is oneself."

Wilde Words

"One can always be kind to people about whom one cares nothing."

Wilde Words

"You might see nothing in him. I see everything in him."

Wilde Words

"Only what is fine, and finely conceived can feed love. But anything will feed hate."

Wilde Words

"I made your sorrow mine also, that you might have help in bearing it."

Wilde Words

"The one charm of the past is that it is the past."

Wilde Words

"It is only the sacred things that are worth touching"

Wilde Words

"Nothing that is worth knowing can be taught"

Wilde Words

"It is absurd to divide people into good and bad. People are either charming or tedious."

Wilde Words

"A burnt child loves the fire."

Wilde Words

"If you want to tell people the truth, make them laugh, otherwise they'll kill you."

Wilde Words

"One must be serious about something, if one wants to have any amusement in life."

Wilde Words

"A mask tells us more than a face."

Wilde Words

"A red rose is not selfish because it wants to be a red rose. It would be horribly selfish if it wanted all the other flowers in the garden to be both red and roses."

Wilde Words

"Everything popular is wrong."

Wilde Words

"What fire does not destroy, it hardens"

Wilde Words

"Life is a nightmare that prevents one from sleeping."

Wilde Words

"Arguments are to be avoided, they are always vulgar and often convincing."

Wilde Words

"All great ideas are dangerous."

Wilde Words

"Yes: I am a dreamer. For a dreamer is one who can only find his way by moonlight, and his punishment is that he sees the dawn before the rest of the world."

Wilde Words

"To get back my youth I would do anything in the world, except take exercise, get up early, or be respectable."

Wilde Words

"Every portrait that is painted with feeling is a portrait of the artist, not of the sitter."

Wilde Words

"The weather is entrancing, but in my heart there is no sun."

Wilde Words

"The only good thing to do with good advice is pass it on;
it is never of any use to oneself."

Wilde Words

"The sky was pure opal now."

Wilde Words

"One has a right to judge a man by the effect he has over his friends."

Wilde Words

"I see when men love women. They give them but a little of their lives. But women when they love give everything."

Wilde Words

"The work of art is to dominate the spectator: the spectator is not to dominate the work of art."

Wilde Words

"Those who see any difference between soul and body have neither."

Wilde Words

"In this world there are only two tragedies. One is not getting what one wants, & the other is getting it."

Wilde Words

"I knew nothing but shadows and I thought them to be real."

Wilde Words

"My own business always bores me to death; I prefer other people's."

Wilde Words

"Genius lasts longer than beauty"

Wilde Words

"The girl never really lived, and so she has never really died."

Wilde Words

"I am sick of women who love one. Women who hate one are much more interesting."

Wilde Words

"Live! Live the wonderful life that is in you! Let nothing be lost upon you. Be always searching for new sensations. Be afraid of nothing."

Wilde Words

"One should always be a little improbable."

Wilde Words

"I asked the question for the best reason possible, for the only reason, indeed, that excuses anyone for asking any question: simple curiosity."

Wilde Words

"How does one cure the soul? Through the senses"

Wilde Words

"Whenever people talk to me about the weather, I always feel quite certain that they mean something else. And that makes me quite nervous."

Wilde Words

"Nowadays most people die of a sort of creeping common sense, and discover when it is too late that the only things one never regrets are one's mistakes."

Wilde Words

"Sometimes, the unnecessary is necessary."

Wilde Words

"I like men who have a future and women who have a past."

Wilde Words

"We women, as some one says, love with our ears, just as you men love with your eyes..."

Wilde Words

"You know more than you think you know, just as you know less than you want to know."

"Ordinary riches can be stolen, real riches cannot. In your soul are infinitely precious things that cannot be taken from you."

Wilde Words

"Who, being loved, is poor?"

Wilde Words

"Each of us has heaven & hell in him…"

Wilde Words

"A bore is someone who deprives you of solitude without providing you with company."

Wilde Words

"The only way to get rid of temptation is to yield to it."

Wilde Words

"What seems to us as bitter trials are often blessings in disguise"

Wilde Words

"Morality, like art, means drawing a line someplace."

Wilde Words

"Education is an admirable thing, but it is well to remember from time to time that nothing that is worth knowing can be taught."

Wilde Words

"Women are meant to be loved, not to be understood."

Wilde Words

"Most people are other people."

Wilde Words

"The moment you understand a great work of art, it's dead for you."

Wilde Words

"I don't want to go to heaven. None of my friends are there."

Wilde Words

"I have a business appointment that I am anxious... to miss."

Wilde Words

"I hope you have not been leading a double life, pretending to be wicked and being good all the time. That would be hypocrisy."

Wilde Words

"Everything in moderation, including moderation."

Wilde Words

"Everything is about sex, except sex"

Wilde Words

"Knowledge would be fatal. It is the uncertainty that charms one. A mist makes things wonderful."

Wilde Words

"It takes great deal of courage to see the world in all its tainted glory, and still to love it."

Wilde Words

"For one moment our lives met, our souls touched."

Wilde Words

"The aim of life is self-development. To realize one's nature perfectly - that is what each of us is here for."

Wilde Words

"I must remember that a good friend is a new world."

Wilde Words

"A kiss may ruin a human life"

Wilde Words

"No man is rich enough to buy back his past."

Wilde Words

"When you really want love you will find it waiting for you."

Wilde Words

"If you don't get everything you want, think of the things you don't get that you don't want."

Wilde Words

"The true mystery of the world is the visible, not the invisible...."

Wilde Words

"They've promised that dreams can come true - but forgot to mention that nightmares are dreams, too."

Wilde Words

"Live! Live the wonderful life that is in you! Let nothing be lost upon you. Be always searching for new sensations. Be afraid of nothing."

Wilde Words

"Never love anyone who treats you like you're ordinary."

Wilde Words

"Every saint has a past, and every sinner has a future."

Wilde Words

"I am sorry I did not stay away longer. I like being missed."

Wilde Words

"No great artist ever sees things as they really are. If he did, he would cease to be an artist."

Wilde Words

"I never put off till tomorrow what I can possibly do - the day after."

Wilde Words

"I love to talk about nothing. It's the only thing I know anything about."

Wilde Words

"If we're always guided by other people's thoughts, what's the point in having our own?"

Wilde Words

"Memory is the diary we all carry about with us."

Wilde Words

"You will always love, and you will always be loved"

Wilde Words

"Punctuality is the thief of time"

Wilde Words

"Ridicule is the tribute paid to the genius by the mediocrities"

Wilde Words

"The art is nothing without the gift. But the gift is nothing without work."

Wilde Words

"You didn't know it then-you know it now."

Wilde Words

"The heart was made to be broken."

Wilde Words

"You don't love someone for their looks, or their clothes, or for their fancy car, but because they sing a song only you can hear."

Wilde Words

"A thing is not necessarily true because a man dies for it."

Wilde Words

"Experience is merely the name men gave to their mistakes."

Wilde Words

"Paradoxically though it may seem, it is none the less true that life imitates art far more than art imitates life."

Wilde Words

"Give a man a mask and he'll tell you the truth."

Wilde Words

"Quotation is a serviceable substitute for wit."

Wilde Words

"You have killed my love. You used to stir my imagination. Now you don't even stir my curiosity."

Wilde Words

"Life has been your art. You have set yourself to music. Your days are your sonnets."

Wilde Words

"It is not what one does that is wrong, but what one becomes as a consequence of it."

Wilde Words

"I have the simplest tastes. I am always satisfied with the best."

Wilde Words

"Spontaneity is a meticulously prepared art"

Wilde Words

"Behind every exquisite thing that existed, there was something tragic."

Wilde Words

"A little sincerity is a dangerous thing, and a great deal of it is absolutely fatal."

Wilde Words

"If you want to be a doormat you have to lay yourself down first."

Wilde Words

"Those who find ugly meanings in beautiful things are corrupt without being charming. This is a fault.

Wilde Words

"I never travel without my diary. One should always have something sensational to read in the train."

Wilde Words

"Everything is going to be fine in the end. If it's not fine it's not the end."

Wilde Words

Afterward

Erica is a writer, photographer, and designer who lives in Georgia. She's written three books, created anthologies for another three, and is working on another secret project. (Stay tuned). She has written voraciously, tenaciously and secretly since she was 7 years old, when she wrote a letter to Santa asking politely for a Barbie Dream House and a black Barbie with three wardrobe options. Santa delivered the goods, and thusly, a passion for writing was born. She was an online vintage clothing retailer for ten years, writing in her spare time, until one summer day, while sourcing at a thrift store, she realized she wanted to slap the bejeezus out of every last person in

Wilde Words

the shop. That was her last day selling vintage clothing. The next day, she sat down at her laptop and began typing.

She likes nature, as long as nature doesn't crawl, fly or wiggle its way into her house. She loves muted colors, but is drawn to vibrant people. She doesn't wear pink, but won't judge you if you do. *To Kill a Mockingbird* is her favorite book, but she's really digging the new Ms. Marvel series. She's quiet until she's not quiet, and then she's the life of the party. She loves her mother, hates humidity (her hair!) and says 'oh, for god's sake, dammit' at least three times a day. You can find her at her website, www.ericageraldmason.com, or say 'hi' on [Instagram](), @ericagmason.